NATIVE WOMEN IN THE AMERICAS

WOMEN'S ISSUES:
GLOBAL TRENDS

WOMEN'S ISSUES:
GLOBAL TRENDS

NATIVE WOMEN IN THE AMERICAS

BY
KENNETH MCINTOSH

Mason Crest Publishers
Philadelphia

Mason Crest Publishers Inc.
370 Reed Road
Broomall, Pennsylvania 19008
(866) MCP-BOOK (toll free)

First printing
1 2 3 4 5 6 7 8 9 10

Library of Congress Cataloging-in-Publication Data

McIntosh, Kenneth, 1959–
  Native women in the Americas / by Kenneth McIntosh.
     p. cm. — (Women's issues, global trends)
  Includes index.
  ISBN 1-59084-862-4   ISBN 1-59084- 856-X (series)
  1. Indian women—Biography. I. Title. II. Series.
  E98.W8M35 2004
  305.48'897'00922—dc22
                           2004009829

Interior design by Michelle Bouch and MK Bassett-Harvey.
Illustrations by Michelle Bouch.
Produced by Harding House Publishing Service, Inc.
Cover design by Benjamin Stewart.
Printed in India.

CONTENTS

INTRODUCTION

by Mary Jo Dudley

The last thirty years have been a time of great progress for women around the world. In some countries, especially where women have more access to education and work opportunities, the relationships between women and men have changed radically. The boundaries between men's roles and women's roles have been crossed, and women are enjoying many experiences that were denied them in past centuries.

But there is still much to be done. On the global stage, women are increasingly the ones who suffer most from poverty. At the same time that they produce 75 to 90 percent of the world's food crops, they are also responsible for taking care of their households. According to the United Nations, in no country in the world do men come anywhere near to spending as much time on housework as women do. This means that women's job opportunities are often extremely limited, contributing to the "feminization of poverty."

In fact, two out of every three poor adults are women. According to the Decade of Women, "Women do two-thirds of the world's work, receive 10 percent of the world's income, and own one percent of the means of production." Women often have no choice but to take jobs that lack long-term security or

adequate pay; many women work in dangerous working conditions or in unprotected home-based industries. This series clearly illustrates how historic events and contemporary trends (such as war, conflicts, and migration) have also contributed to women's loss of property and diminished access to resources.

A recent report from Human Rights Watch indicates that many countries continue to deny women basic legal protections. Amnesty International points out, "Governments are not living up to their promises under the Women's Convention to protect women from discrimination and violence such as rape and female genital mutilation." Many nations—including the United States—have not ratified the United Nations' Women's Treaty.

During times of armed conflict, especially under policies of ethnic cleansing, women are particularly at risk. Murder, torture, systematic rape, forced pregnancy, and forced abortions are all too common human rights violations endured by women around the world. This series presents the experience of women in Vietnam, Cambodia, the Middle East, and other war-torn regions.

In the political arena, equality between men and women has still not been achieved. Around the world, women are underrepresented in their local and national governments; on average, women represent only 10 percent of all legislators worldwide. This series provides excellent examples of key female leaders who have promoted women's rights and occupied unique leadership positions, despite historical contexts that would normally have shut them out from political and social prominence.

The Fourth World Conference on Women called upon the international community to take action in the following areas of concern:

- the persistent and increasing burden of poverty on women
- inequalities and inadequacies in access to education and training
- inequalities and inadequacies in access to health care and related services
- violence against women

- the effects of armed or other kinds of conflict on women
- inequality in economic structures and policies, in all forms of productive processes, and in access to resources
- insufficient mechanisms at all levels to promote the advancement of women
- lack of protection of women's human rights
- stereotyping of women and inequality in women's participation in all community systems, especially the media
- gender inequalities in the management of natural resources and the safe-guarding of the environment
- persistent discrimination against and violation of the rights of female children

The Conference's mission statement includes these sentences: "Equality between women and men is a matter of human rights and a condition for social justice and is also a necessary and fundamental prerequisite for equality, development and peace . . . equality between women and men is a condition . . . for society to meet the challenges of the twenty-first century." This series provides examples of how women have risen above adversity, despite their disadvantaged social, economic, and political positions.

Each book in WOMEN'S ISSUES: GLOBAL TRENDS takes a look at women's lives in a different key region or culture, revealing the history, contributions, triumphs, and challenges of women around the world. Women play key roles in shaping families, spirituality, and societies. By interweaving historic backdrops with the modern-day evolving role of women in the home and in society at large, this series presents the important part women play as cultural communicators. Protection of women's rights is an integral part of universal human rights, peace, and economic security. As a result, readers who gain understanding of women's lives around the world will have deeper insight into the current condition of global interactions.

GRANDMOTHERS' WAYS: NATIVE WOMEN'S HISTORICAL AND CONTINUING TRADITIONS

Long ago, the girl named Nomtaimet and her band of Wintu people lived in what is today central California. The land provided acorns and game, while the ocean yielded abundant fish. The people lived well. Nomtaimet's parents were wise and honorable.

When Nomtaimet reached the age when her body changed to become a woman, she and her parents followed the appropriate custom. Nomtaimet went to a special hut, apart from the rest of her village. Only her mother and grandmother spent time with her. They washed and brushed her hair, and brought her meals. Most important, they spent days telling her what it means to be a woman. Nomtaimet listened carefully to all she was told. She learned by heart all the ways of her ancestors.

When winter had passed, she was ready to be presented to the people—she was now a woman. The band prepared a feast. Delectable dishes of game, berries, and nuts were prepared. Special clothes were sewn for Nomtaimet—a buckskin skirt, strings of colorful shells, and beads. A sacred willow staff was carved to honor her. When she emerged from her hut, everyone was delighted.

The indigenous women of Guatemala show the power of traditions to survive, despite more than five hundred years of opposition from the outside world.

NATIVE WOMEN IN THE AMERICAS

From head to toe, she radiated beauty—the beauty of an honorable, dignified woman. The people stood to honor her.

Someone said, "It's time to do the circle dance." From the beginning of the world, the circle dance has honored the day when a girl becomes a woman. The whole village began to shuffle their feet, sing, and dance in a great circle. From other villages, more people arrived to join in the dance.

For ten days, they danced and ate, ate and danced. At the end of the changing ceremony, they all said what a wonderful time it was and what an honorable young woman was Nomtaimet. They had never seen a young woman like her. The people were so joyful they kept on dancing. They danced all the way up the trail to the next village, where more joined them. Then they danced over hills and through streams to the next village, and the next. They danced so hard their clothes fell off. They painted themselves and danced on. They danced through all four seasons. They danced all around the whole world.

Finally, they arrived back at the village where the dance had begun, and the dancing stopped. Yet the people never forgot what a wonderful celebration they had shared in honor of a special young woman.

The Wintu, like all Native people, have sacred traditions, which teach the meaning of life. These could be compared to the Jewish or Christian Bible, except they have been passed down through time by word of mouth, rather than pieces of paper. Nomtaimet's sacred tale defines the values of the Wintu. Her celebration shows how important girls are, and what honor and joy they experience when they reach womanhood.

No one is certain how many people lived in the Americas when Europeans began their invasion in 1492, but the average guess is around 50,000,000. From the Yagan people of Tierra del Fuego, the southern tip of South America, to the Gwich'in, dwelling along the northernmost shores of the Arctic plains, hundreds of distinct cultures thrived on this continent. Indigenous women's lives varied greatly from one culture to the next. Sometimes there was considerable variety of women's roles even within the same tribe.

As you read this book, beware of generalizing. What's true of one Native group may be the opposite of another. In some cases, ancient traditions have been lost under the onslaught of white people's ways. Yet in countless ways, the vital traditional beliefs and practices of Native people continue today.

Many Indian nations have traditions like the dance of Nomtaimet, showing how women should be honored. For the Oceti Sakowin, White Buffalo Calf Woman appeared, bringing with her the sacred pipe, which established peace and truth for the people. The Cherokee say they come from Corn Mother, who cut open her breast so that corn could spring forth and sustain the people. Throughout the Americas, sacred traditions emphasize the importance of

"All Indian nations always held women in high honor and respect. It is a mystery how stories of Indian women being the slaves, so to speak, of our society ever got started and why these false stories persist. It is time the false stories end that say Indian men do not hold their women in high esteem."

—Long Standing Bear Chief, Blackfoot writer, educator, and lecturer.

This young Apache woman, photographed by Edward Curtis a century ago, is dressed as Changing Woman for her Sunrise Dance Ceremony. Today's Apache girls wear similar attire for this special event.

Mother Earth. The Hopi and Zuni, in New Mexico and Arizona, recall how they emerged into the world through a Sipapu—Mother Earth's birth canal.

Traditionally, women's reproductive powers were viewed as mysterious and sacred. Today, Apache girls at the time of their first menstruation still celebrate with a traditional Sunrise Dance, or Puberty Ceremony. The girl in the ceremony becomes Changing Woman, who was the mother of all people and represents all the powers of women through the ages. Preparations for the ceremony can take months. More than a third of Apache girls choose to have such a ceremony, even though it involves several days of rigorous ritual disciplines. As she becomes Changing Woman, the girl acquires supernatural powers to bring blessing to those who attend her ceremony. The Sunrise Dance gives young women a strong sense of worth, along with the responsibility of their new biological abilities.

Old-time customs accompanying childbirth varied greatly. In some tribes, birth took place in the woman's own dwelling. Groups, such as the Crow, prepared a special lodge set apart just for the occasion. Other groups set aside special places outdoors near their village for childbirth. Older women with experience in delivery usually assisted in the birth. In most cultures, men were kept away from the event. Nowadays, most North American Indians choose to give birth in hospitals or with professional midwives.

Among the Kwakiutl, of British Columbia, Canada, births in past times took place outdoors in fair weather and inside the wood longhouse during the winter months. Two older women of the tribe were designated as *midwives*, and they would assist with the delivery. The pregnant woman sat on the edge of a pit dug in the ground and lined with soft cedar bark to receive the new child in comfort. The midwives were skilled in their craft, able to handle medical situations like a *breech birth* and well schooled to give emotional help for the mother as well. Kwakiutl mothers were kept in bed resting for four days following the birth.

"Our ancestors considered it a great offense to reject the counsels of their women, especially of their female leaders. They were esteemed the mistresses of the soil. Who, said they, bring us into being? Who cultivates our land, kindles our fires, but our women?"
—Domine Pater, Seneca-Cayuga orator, in a 1788 speech to the governor of New York.

In the old days, women of the woodlands, Great Plains, and Western Basin carried their infants in cradleboards. The cradleboard could be considered the forerunner of today's plastic baby carrier. Cradleboard frames were made sturdily of wood, and often decorated with lavish beadwork or quillwork. Cradleboards are some of the finest examples of Native women's art. The interiors were lined with furs or grass for comfort. The cradleboard could be carried on the back by straps, or securely hung on branches or lodge poles. This enabled mothers to go about their tasks, farming, preparing food, and so on, with their little ones. Babies were cuddled and cared for, but as soon as they were able to receive education, elders began to teach them how to perform all the tasks needed for adulthood.

Clans form the basis of many Native cultures. The clan is a sort of "super family," very important for a sense of identity and place in the larger community. Where European cultures relied on the immediate family to provide a child's care and training, Indian children could rely on a broad network of people to look after them. This provided them with values and a sense of belonging based on the community as a whole. In Native North American communities today, schools and day care centers have somewhat replaced the traditional roles of the extended family, yet clan traditions remain important.

Some Native cultures are matrilineal. That means inheritance of family name is passed down from the mother's side of the family. Other Indian cultures, especially those traditionally based on hunting, trace inheritance through the fathers.

"Where are your women?"

—the astonished query by Cherokee chief Ostenaco, on meeting with British government representatives to make a treaty, astonished that white women were not involved in such an important decision.

In some ancient American cultures, women held great authority. The Spaniard de Soto, exploring what is today South Carolina, encountered a chief of the Cofitachequi people. One of de Soto's companions remarked, "We traveled through her lands for hundreds of leagues, in which, as we saw, she was very well obeyed, for all the Indians did with great efficiency and diligence what she ordered of them."

Not all the first nations gave women such power. According to an ancient Spanish record, the Florentine Codex, baby Aztec girls were told at birth, "You will be in the heart of the home, you will go nowhere. Here your lord plants and buries you. You will become fatigued, tired; you are to provide water, to grind maize; you are to sweat by the ashes of the hearth." Men's freedom was greater than women's in Aztec society, since it relied so heavily on the military power of its warriors.

In most Indian societies in the old days, women's work was strenuous. Beverly Hungry Wolf, of the Blood People of Canada's Blackfoot Nation, in her book *The Ways of My Grandmothers*, shares thoughts on this worth:

Actually, when you judge the traditional lives of my grandmothers by modern values you could, indeed, say that they had hard lives and were much mistreated. The modern woman would rebel against carrying loads of firewood home in the middle of a cold winter while her husband sat inside the house smoking and entertaining his friends. Yet my grandmothers did it for as long as they could walk, and they were not known to complain.... But my grandfathers, in turn, spent countless frozen days and nights out on those same cold winter days, seeking food to kill and bring home; or defending their families from prowling enemies. . . . Times have changed so much that we can barely imagine the daily challenges faced by our forefathers. For that reason it is pretty hard to make any judgments about the ways they did things.

In remote regions of the Andes, many of Peru's Quechua Indian women live lives very similar to their Inca ancestors five hundred years ago. Rural native villages have a strong sense of community, and today's Quechua women continue to support one another as they struggle against poverty and discrimination.

NATIVE WOMEN IN THE AMERICAS

Some Native societies practiced *polygamy* in the old days. Virginia Driving Hawk Sneve, in her book *Completing the Circle*, comments on the practice among the Lakota. She points out that several wives in a household made everyone's work lighter. Furthermore, she says, "the more women in the lodge, the more they controlled the man." Unhappy wives could take their personal items and children and leave the husband's lodge. Women in many tribes owned their own property and were free to divorce for any reason without being looked down upon. Multiple wives are only a historical memory in North America, but the practice continues among some isolated Indian populations in Mexico and South America.

While there were clear differences between men and women in traditional Indian cultures in terms of dress, customs, and responsibilities, they were also able to accept people who chose to live outside of expected roles. Running Eagle, of the Blackfoot Nation, was famous for her exploits as a warrior. She became a chief, based on her successes in battle, and male warriors followed her willingly into armed conflict. A widowed woman and her siblings took care of the domestic duties in her lodge so Running Eagle could follow men's ways.

Leslie Marmon Silko of Laguna, in her book *Yellow Woman and Beauty of the Spirit*, observes,

> In the old Pueblo world, differences were celebrated as a sign of the Mother Creator's grace. People born with exceptional physical or sexual differences were highly respected and honored because their physical differences gave them special positions as mediators between this world and the spirit world.

This fit well with a culture where "beauty was manifested in behavior and in one's relationships with other living beings. Beauty was . . . a feeling of harmony."

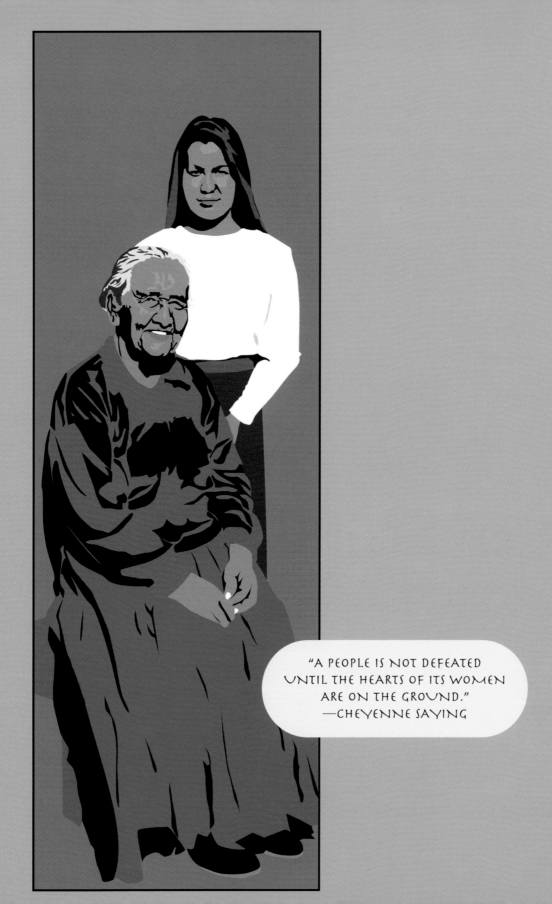

UNDEFEATED HEARTS: NATIVE WOMEN, HISTORY, AND CULTURAL SURVIVAL

In February of 2003, Adelina Fontes, a forty-four-year-old Tarahumara woman, along with four companions, walked unarmed onto a dirt road deep in the Sierra Madre Mountains in the State of Chihuahua, Mexico. They were right in the path of logging trucks bound for the state capital. For too long they had allowed logging trucks to carry away the trees—destroying forests the Tarahumara depend upon for survival.

For centuries, the Tarahumara have dwelt in the canyons of the Sierra Madre, living a practically stone-age existence secluded from the larger world. That changed in recent decades, however. Drug lords and loggers have taken over this isolated region of Mexico, threatening the Tarahumara environment and culture.

Soon, word of the women's blockade spread. Many other women joined the five. Among them was Chana Torres, who at thirty had been widowed twice by local violence. The truckers tried to force their way through, saying that a local narcotics *trafficker* would enforce their right to go through. If the protesters had been men, the truckers said, they would have run over them.

This news story, reported by D'Ann Johnson in the *Texas Observer*, is just the latest chapter in a long history of Native women who have stood against threatening outside forces. For five hundred years, Indian women have resisted relentless attacks on their cultures, lands, and ways. The continuing vitality of hundreds of Native nations in the Americas is a tribute to women's strength and determination.

When Columbus landed on the shores of this continent, he called the Native people "Indians." This was likely due to his mistaken belief he had reached India. If he had assumed it was China, would we be calling Native people today "Chinese"? Russel Means, a Lakota *activist*, claims the world "Indian" comes from Columbus saying the Native people were "en Dios"—meaning they were "in God," or naturally spiritual. Today, some people speak of "First Nations" peoples, or Native Americans. Others prefer the simple term "Indian." Many prefer to use the name of their tribe for identification.

Ray Fadden, a Mohawk educator, says the lifestyle of most North Americans today has more in common with the lives of Native people than of Europeans at the time of their arrival. We eat potatoes, corn, beans, and numerous other foods first cultivated on this continent. Common medicines that save thousands of lives today were known to Native healers long ago. The game of putting a bouncing rubber ball through a hoop is a gift from the Indians of Central America. The United States' government, with two groups of representatives, is patterned after the Haudenosaunee (or Iroquois) confederacy.

While Caucasian newcomers to this continent benefited from cultural exchange, the *indigenous* inhabitants suffered enormously. Scholars have referred to the European invasion of the Americas as genocide—the deliberate attempt by one group of people to utterly obliterate the lives and culture of others. Records show that by 1650, only 6 million Indians remained in all of North America, South America, and the Caribbean. In only 150 years, more than 44 million people perished.

This Teton Sioux woman, photographed by Edward Curtis in 1908, lived during an especially hard time for North American Indian women. At this low point in their history, Indian women began speaking and writing to inform people of their plight.

Paintings and photographs made by non-Natives—such as this photograph by Edward Curtis—have tended to romanticize Native women rather than show the way they really lived.

"The Indians survived our open intentions of wiping them out, and since the tide turned they have even weathered our good intentions toward them, which can be much more deadly."

—John Steinbeck, **American and the Americans**

History records numerous examples of massacres committed by Spanish, English, and American armies from the arrival of Columbus until recent decades. One such event took place at Wounded Knee, South Dakota, in 1890. Oglala tribal member American Horse recounted what he saw: "Right near the flag of truce a mother was shot down with her infant. The women as they were fleeing with their babes were killed together, shot right through, and women who were very heavy with child were also killed." When the shooting stopped, more than 150 Indians had been killed, mostly women and children. Participating soldiers were awarded medals of honor.

While many Native people were killed by violence, even more perished from disease. Lacking immunity to European illnesses, entire indigenous nations were wiped out by *smallpox* and other sicknesses. At least in one case, this was intentional. In 1763, British General Lord Jeffrey Amherst instructed one of

his officers to infect Indians by means of smallpox-infested blankets. Colonel Henry Bouquet replied that he would do so, "taking care however not to disease myself." Started with a "gift" of germ-laden blankets and handkerchiefs, a smallpox *epidemic* spread among the Shawnee, Mingo, and Huron nations.

Even when Europeans have not desired to spread disease, Indian populations have been ravaged by illnesses after contact with Europeans. Patrick Tierney, in his book *Darkness in El Dorado*, gives heart-wrenching accounts of illnesses that continue to kill Native people today in the Amazon. He says, "a third or more of Amazonian Natives die in the five years after first contact [with whites]." The book is a grim documentation of the ways *anthropologists*, miners, and government workers destroy groups of people, even as they seek to learn about them.

From the time of their arrival, Europeans *stereotyped* Native women. They were sometimes idealized as the "Indian princess," a beautiful and exotic (or

"If Columbus could discover a country that was already occupied, I can go into the parking lot and discover your car—with you in it."
—Comedian Dick Gregory

erotic) female who invited Europeans to come and take her riches. Pocahontas is a historical woman who was portrayed in this mythic form. On the other extreme, Caucasian settlers looked down on Native women as "squaws." Today the word "squaw" has become an insult implying women are beasts of burden and the property of men.

The leadership roles of women in Indian societies were eroded by contact with white society. The *conquistador* Sepulvada believed that, "women are to men as infants are to adults." White officials refused to honor Native women's leadership. Indians, at the same time, were puzzled by the complete absence of women in European decision making.

Shortly after Columbus came to the Americas, Spanish sailors began the trans-Atlantic sex trade. Native girls captured in the Americas were taken to

Hopi artist Nampeyo, photographed by Edward Curtis in 1906, attracted national attention for her refinement of ancient Pueblo pottery forms.

Europe and sold as prostitutes. In the colonies, Indian women who had been stolen or purchased served as slaves and sexual partners. Some Native women allied themselves with traders in order to gain preferential treatment for their tribes. Cherokee author Rayna Green, in her book *Women in American Indian Society*, says:

> Disease and demoralization killed millions, but the sexual conquest of North America actually secured a cultural victory over Native peoples. The creation of an enormous mixed-blood population changed forever the nature of Indian societies.

Education was another tool of conquest. Beginning in the nineteenth century, white people built Indian boarding schools. These institutions aimed to "save the child by killing the Indian" inside of them. Students were taken from their families, placed in unfamiliar settings with children of other tribes, and punished for speaking their Native language or practicing traditional ways. An Acoma clan mother recalls the day when her brother arrived at the boarding school she attended and informed her she could legally leave the school and go home. She packed her things and walked out the door at once.

Indian women, long regarded as the ones who guaranteed their people's future, were instrumental in the renewal of their people, beginning in the late nineteenth century. Sarah Winnemucca, a Paiute, lived through a series of government attempts to starve and confine her people. Educated in a mission school, Winnemucca went on lecture tours. She won over large audiences with her mesmerizing speeches in her people's defense. Winnemucca once said, "If women could get into your congress, I think justice would soon be done to the Indians." Susan LaFlesche, of the Omaha tribe, became the first female American Indian physician. She combated illnesses that afflicted the Omaha and also spoke at public gatherings, arguing against government corruption and harmful policies. Emily Pauline Johnson, daughter of an Englishwoman and a

Mohawk chief, was an actor, poet, and speaker. She wrote and spoke eloquently for mutual respect between the races in Canada. At the turn of the century, Hopi artist Nampeyo gained national fame for refining traditional forms of Pueblo pottery.

In the twentieth century, Native women were able to see the *revitalization* of their communities and renewal of traditional ways as their efforts in education, politics, and the arts came to fruition. Artist Maria Martinez, of San

Guatemala's Native women continue their struggle for physical and cultural survival. These women are selling wares in an open-air marketplace in Chi Chi Castenango.

NATIVE WOMEN IN THE AMERICAS

Ildefonso Pueblo, gained worldwide fame for her pottery. Sioux linguist Ella Deloria and Okanogan scholar Cristal Quintasket preserved Native languages and oral traditions.

In the 1970s, Native women rode a wave of cultural renewal and political activism. In Canada, Indian women's *advocacy* groups gained reform of the Indian acts, which had previously deprived women who married non-Indians of their tribal membership. Women in the United States were in the forefront of Indian activist groups like the American Indian Movement.

Women gained power for their tribal nations by working as *Environmentalists, lobbyists*, and politicians. Wilma Mankiller became the chief of the Cherokee nation in Oklahoma, and has successfully worked to rejuvenate the economy and social power of her nation. As the millenium approached, women were voted in as chiefs in more than a dozen Indian nations.

In Guatemala, Mayan Indians in the highlands continue their struggle for physical and cultural survival. In the 1980s, government troops massacred Indian villages. Although such violent killings have stopped, Mayans continue to die by starvation and suffer from malnutrition. Rigoberta Menchu published an autobiographical account of the Mayan people's suffering, and in 1992 she won the Nobel Peace Prize for her work.

In 1992, quoted in *Native Peoples* magazine, Wilma Mankiller summed up the state of Indian nations. She said, "Despite the last 500 years, there is still much to celebrate. . . . Our languages are still strong, ceremonies that we have been conducting since the beginning of time are still being held, . . . most importantly, we continue to exist as a distinct cultural group in the midst of the most powerful country in the world." She is well aware of the problems continuing to face American Indians—low education, poverty, and racism. At the same time, she looks to the future with optimism. "We look forward to the next 500 years as a time of renewal and revitalization for Native people throughout North America."

"NOW I AM LONG LIFE,
NOW HAPPINESS. . . .
BEHIND ME BLESSING IS
EXTENDED TO THE MOUNTAINS. . . .
BELOW ME BLESSING IS
EXTENDED TO THE SKY
AS WITH THE AID OF A
BEAUTIFUL ONE I WALK ABOUT."
—NAVAJO BLESSINGWAY
CEREMONY SONG

SACRED PATHS:
NATIVE WOMEN'S SPIRITUALITY TODAY

"I cried during the entire ceremony. Tears are the highest form of prayer," Henrietta Mann stated, recalling the healing ceremony she conducted at Ground Zero, former site of the World Trade Center, following the horrifying attacks of September 11, 2001. Mann and her daughter, Montoya Whiteman, both Cheyenne prayer women, were the first of several Indian spiritual leaders the Red Cross Spiritual Care Center brought to Ground Zero. The *Montana State University News Service* reported on their visit. As the Cheyenne women began their ceremony, those laboring to retrieve bodies and remove wreckage stopped the noise of their work to watch.

Mann lit her smudge pot, a small vessel filled with burning sage, and said a prayer to each of the four directions. "My prayers were for the healing of earth," she said. "And for the people working in the pit. And I prayed that the great-grandchildren of our great-grandchildren will never have to experience a tragedy of this kind."

Even though her ancestors also suffered violence, Mann says it is hard to understand such hatred. She says, "It is important in this holy season that we pray for peace, for love, whether it is for ourselves, or for other people."

Throughout the Americas, First Nations women continue the spiritual beliefs and customs of their ancient ancestors. At the same time, many have embraced Christianity—either in its Catholic or Protestant forms. Some Indians feel Christianity is incompatible with traditional Native religion. A Jicarilla Apache woman, who has studied other religions but is committed to traditional spiritual beliefs, says, "It is hypocrisy to say you honor the ten commandments, which say you must only worship one deity, and then attend a bear dance ceremony." On the other side, Pentecostal Christians require members to separate from traditional spiritual practices.

"The Creator, Maker of all things, gave woman the power of the pipe. We pray with the pipe so we might worship in the proper way. The pipe, this female gift, is our assurance of a long, happy and healthy life. If it were not for women, our ceremonial life, as we know it today, would not exist."
—Long Standing Bear Chief, Blackfoot

The spiritual values that sustained Native women in the past are being instilled in a new generation.

Other Indians, especially in the southwestern American pueblos and parts of Mexico and Central America, claim allegiance to both Christianity and traditional beliefs. As one clan mother of the Acomas put it: "Acomas are 98 percent Catholic—and 100 percent traditional." A San Juan and Hopi Indian, Bernadett Gallegos, explains, "As we hold dual citizenship as United States citizens and as members of our particular villages, we also hold dear our two faiths—that of our ancestors and that of the faith brought to us over four hundred years ago."

Traditional spiritual beliefs are incredibly varied, though some generalizations can be made. In Native thought, the worlds of humans, animals, and

In Cholula, Mexico, the Spanish conquistadors built a Christian church atop an Aztec pyramid. The church overlooks a site where Spanish soldiers massacred Native people.

"We are told that when the Inca Manco fought the Spanish at the time of the coming of the whites, he said this to the indigenous people: 'Do not forget the rituals of your ancestors . . . do what you have to in public, but in private keep our old customs and ceremonies close to your hearts.' And this we still do."
—a Quechua Indian speaking to author Michael Wood, at a traditional ceremony in Peru, year 2000

inanimate nature are not separated as they are in European religions. The "two-legged beings" and the "four-legged beings" along with the natural elements are all regarded as equals in the natural and spiritual world. Special reverence is given to Mother Earth.

For many Native traditions, the word "religion" isn't really appropriate. The term "religion" assumes a set of beliefs and practices that are separated from ordinary, *secular* existence. First Nations people point out that their spiritual beliefs cannot be separated from everyday, ordinary life. As one Apache woman

explains, "Jicarilla spiritual beliefs are your whole life. Harmony is what matters—not going to a special house for worship or observing your religion on one special day, but how you live day to day."

Daily prayers and gestures accompany the everyday experience of Native spirituality. Traditional Haudenosaunee (Iroquois) people begin each day by reciting the "Words that come before all else." This prayer gives thanks to the Creator and to all the elements of the natural world. Daily thanksgiving helps keep "a good mind"—a constant attitude of gratitude and peace. Likewise, many Pueblo Indians make corn offerings to their ancestors at each day's start and at suppertime. They reflect on how their actions affect Mother Earth, the Creator, and their ancestors. This helps them keep a "good heart," maintaining harmony within themselves and with others through the day.

Most North American Indians choose not to discuss traditional spirituality with outsiders. They have good reason for their reluctance. How would you feel if someone entered the place you worship and stole sacred ceremonial objects? Would you like it if complete strangers barged into the most important ceremony of your life—say your First Communion or Bar Mitzvah—talking loudly, taking flash photographs, and rudely asking questions that interrupted the ritual? All these things have happened as non-Native tourists, scientists, art collectors, *New-Agers*, and others have violated Indian spiritual observances. Native people have learned that privacy is the best protection for their spiritual lives.

In North America, younger generations are increasingly turning back to traditional spirituality. Mandy Begay, an Apache, shares on a Web site her experience:

Ever since I was old enough to understand the meaning of the Sunrise Dance, I was told that it was essential for me as a growing woman to have one. I hated the idea. . . . I felt it was only some stupid ritual. . . . Therefore,

Spiritual power is bestowed on a young woman during the Sunrise Dance ceremony.

it came to me as a surprise when I had strong feelings while I partici-
pated in one as an assistant for my friend Laura's Sunrise Dance.

Midway through the ceremony, she says, "The singers sang louder and
louder of our Apache ways, love, and friendship. I didn't understand all the
words, but I knew what they said. They were telling me to be strong in life and
to live life to its fullest. The louder they sang, the harder I danced." She con-
cludes by saying:

As I stood along the sidelines and watched Laura dance, I imagined it was my dance. I was the one changing into a woman. I was the one with all the strength, and I was the one with the respect from my elders for continuing the tradition. My desire to be a Sunrise Dance girl grew in the matter of a morning, but by this time, it was too late for me to have one.

For five centuries, missionaries have urged Native people to transfer their allegiance to Christ. Such invitations were often accompanied by forced relocation, forced labor, and attempts to destroy Indian languages and customs. Such tactics only increased resistance to the new faith. In some cases, the Christian gospel was more willingly received. The Lagunas had an ancient prophecy that a man would come to them with the sign of a cross—so they were receptive in

"The Navajo's concept of religion is so total that it can be said that there is no such thing as religion in Navajo culture because everything is religious. Everything a Navajo knows—his shelter, his fields, his livestock, the sky above him and the ground on which he walks—is holy."
—Raymond Friday Locke, **The Book of the Navajo**

1699 when a Franciscan Friar carrying a crucifix arrived and asked to live among them. Today, Catholic churches stand in all the pueblos, in most Canadian Indian communities, and throughout Latin America.

In Guatemala and Chiapas, Mexico, Mayan people combined their traditional beliefs with the new faith. Their love for the earth goddess was transferred to the Virgin Mother. The Maya Tree of Life, a maize stalk representing new life, became a crucifix. Throughout Mexico and Central America, Catholic churches were erected atop sacred pyramids. As Bill Weinberg puts it in his book *Homage to Chiapas*, "For the Maya, the masks of Christ and the Virgin were thin." Sacrifices of corn and slaughtered chickens are still left in Mayan highland churches, honoring Christ and the Virgin with the same offerings given their predecessors.

Catholic Indian women in Latin America feel special attachment to the Virgin of Guadalupe. According to tradition, the Virgin appeared to Indian peasant Juan Diego in 1531 just outside what is now Mexico City. The Virgin was dark-skinned and spoke to Diego in his native Indian language. The Church has declared the appearance to be genuine, and Pope John Paul II declared Juan Diego a saint. This appearance by the Virgin was one of the most important factors in the massive conversion of Mexican Indians to the Catholic Church.

Kateri Tekakwitha has not yet been declared a saint, but she is immensely popular with Catholic Indian women in North America. The daughter of a Mohawk chief, Kateri was born in upstate New York in 1656. Missionaries came to her village, and she was baptized at the age of eighteen. She was deeply devoted to her new faith. Six years later, she died of disease. Her last words were "Christ, I love you." In 1980, the Catholic Church beatified her (one step below being declared a saint). Indian churches in Albuquerque, the pueblos of New Mexico, the Navajo Nation in Arizona, and the six Haudenosaunee (Iroquois) nations in New York and Canada have statues of Kateri. She may be dressed in

Many of Guatemala's Mayan Indians are Catholic, but their religious traditions contain many elements from their ancient spiritual beliefs. Here, in a celebration of the Feast of San Jose, the air is white with burning copal, a resin from Central and South American trees.

handmade garments typical of the local tribe. Corn offerings are sometimes left at her feet. There are women's Kateri Societies throughout Indian Country, dedicated to increasing her popularity.

Some Native women choose to forsake the old traditions of indigenous beliefs and Catholicism, in order to embrace Protestant forms of Christianity. The Pentecostal or Charismatic churches are especially common among Native peoples throughout the Americas. Pentecostal Christians stress the importance of a personal *conversion* experience, the authority of the Bible, and worship that involves speaking in unknown languages, or "tongues."

The acceptance of Protestant Christianity comes with a cost, for it causes a break with the traditional spirituality of Native people. For some, the benefits are worth it. One Indian woman shares on an Internet site her spiritual journey:

> God intervened in my life. Before I was a hurting person, wounded and depressed turning to alcohol and other things. . . . I was a mess. . . . But God reached me, picked me up, cleaned me up, set me free. Miracles do happen.

Today's Native women follow a great variety of faiths. In some cases, allegiance to one belief or the other may earn the disapproval of family and friends, or may even threaten division in Indian communities. Whether they follow ancient Native ways, or Catholicism, or the newer Christian groups, Indian women in each tradition serve as examples and pillars of spirituality. As Beverly Hungry Wolf recalls in *The Ways of My Grandmothers*, "All of my traditional grandmothers prayed a lot and believed in their religion. To me they were all holy women."

"IN OUR SOCIETY, WOMEN ARE THE CENTER OF ALL THINGS. NATURE, WE BELIEVE, HAS GIVEN WOMEN THE ABILITY TO CREATE; THEREFORE IT IS ONLY NATURAL THAT WOMEN BE IN POSITIONS OF POWER TO PROTECT THIS FUNCTION."
—DOUG GEORGE-KANANTIIO

4

UNBREAKABLE BONDS

"In October of 1951 Wari:so:se passed into the spirit world in a way that caused great sorrow for her family but was marked with dignity, self-sacrifice and honor." With these words, Doug George-Kanentiio pays tribute to his grandmother in his book, *Iroquois Culture and Commentary*. Before coming to this end, she had lived a full life. Wari:so:se—Josephine was her English name—had nine children with her husband Jacob George. There was no welfare system, nor reservation distribution of casino moneys at that time. She did whatever she could to provide for her family: scaled fish, smoked meat, and spent hours by the light of a gas lamp sewing clothes for her children.

One fateful day in 1951, she was helping her daughter care for a newborn granddaughter. A fire broke out in the apartment building where the daughter lived. Wari:so:se was told to leave, but she would not leave the burning apartment without the baby. She reached the child, but the fire had cut off her escape. She called out a window, and when rescuers were in place, she carefully dropped her granddaughter to them and then jumped. The granddaughter landed safely, but Wari:so:se perished in the fall. She is one of countless Native mothers who gave of herself unselfishly for her family and community.

Women elders are especially honored in many tribes.

Among the six nations of the Haudenosaunee (Iroquois), elders and mothers are given special honor. In white North American culture, a boy who speaks too highly of his mother or seems unduly attached to her might suffer being called a "mama's boy." Not so among the Haudenosaunee. Mothers, aunts, and grandmothers are highly esteemd by men of all ages. Givers and nurturers of life, they are revered, even as Mother Earth is revered for the way she maintains all of life. The mother determines family relationships. If a mother is a member of a tribal nation, then her children share the same membership. If the mother is not a member of the tribe, even if the father is, the children will not be.

Halfway across the United States, west of Albuquerque, New Mexico, the Laguna Nation lives in their Pueblo villages. The desert landscape looks very different from the woodland of the Northeast where the Haudenosaunee dwell. Yet the Lagunas share the same sort of esteem for their mothers and female

REALLY BIG FAMILY

Within a Laguna Pueblo clan, all members of the same generation are "brother" or "sister" to one another. Also, aunts are called "mother," signifying their role in raising their nieces and nephews.

elders. When Veronica and Candice Sarracino are asked who their hero is, both answer, "Our mother." She is a role model, and a source of strength for the entire family. Veronica and Candice are sisters living in the village of Mesita. Like many Pueblo Indians, three generations live together in the Sarracino house. Their aunts also live near and are highly valued. The Laguna word for "aunt" is the same as the word for "mother," because aunts play an important role in raising their nieces and nephews.

In addition to their family connections, the Sarracinos also have deep roots in their clans. Clans, or groups of families, are the basic social units among the Pueblo, Navajo, and Haudenosaunee Indians, along with many other Native nations. Clan membership in these nations is traced through the mother's side

THERE'S NO PLACE LIKE HOME

"Land and family make Indian people who they are; they give them an absolute sense of home. Millie Touchin, from Laguna Pueblo, puts this simply and strongly: 'Some people don't have a place, a beginning. We're lucky. We have something and somebody.'"

—Stephen Trimble, **The People**

Today, schools and daycare centers perform some of the services provided by parents and clans.

of the family. A person is "big clan" on the mother's side, and "little clan" on the father's side. The origins of the clans go back in time to the Ancient Ancestors. Clans are named after animals or natural forces: eagle, antelope, turtle, bear, deer, corn, sun, sky, and so on. When Native people are getting acquainted, it is

Women hold positions of respect and pride in many Native communities.

common to ask, "What clan are you?" Clans also help people to know how to behave properly. If a clan member behaves badly, the whole group is disgraced. One of the saddest things one Navajo can say of another is: "He acts as if he has no relatives."

When Indian young men and women from clan-based societies meet and like each other, the first thing they want to know is: "What clan are you?" Within a clan, all members are "brother" or "sister" to one another. For this reason, one must not marry within one's clan. The Navajo have more than seventy clans, and have added clans for children descended from Mexican, Anglo, African, or Asian parents.

The Iroquois and Pueblo cultures are matriarchal; that is, women hold power in the social system. Women are very important because of their place in the clans, though men have traditionally held political office. At Acoma, the youngest daughter in a family owns all the family property, since the youngest daughter will live longest and gain the most wisdom. So when the family property needs repair, or is going to be rented, the brothers have to ask the youngest sister for her approval before anything is done.

The leadership of the Haudenosaunee nations, and of Acoma Pueblo, is also matriarchal. Clan mothers appoint tribal officers. If they disapprove of their actions, the women can also remove council members. Men do the works of government yet serve at the pleasure of the clan mothers. At Acoma, the women of the Antelope clan appoint tribal officers: the Governor, Lieutenant Governor, Secretary, Treasurer, and so on. They may be removed from office if the clan mothers perceive them failing in their duties.

The Pueblo Indians today are strongly connected to family, clan, and community. This enables people of all ages to experience a sense of belonging, support, and community strength, which many non-Indians have never experienced. If someone has a medical need, or lacks housing, they have their clan to fall back on. If children or adolescents get into trouble, other community

STURDY FOUNDATION

The Apaches say, "Mothers are the trunk of the family tree, children are its branches, and husbands are the leaves. The leaves may break off, but the trunk and the branches never break."

members hear of it, so problems with young people can be addressed without needing to involve the law.

Among the majority of First Nations in North America, traditional patterns of child rearing have changed much in the past decade. In old times, parents were responsible for teaching everything to their children. Mothers would spend most of their time with daughters. Now, pressures to earn money have forced many young mothers to work during the day. In today's Indian communities, a whole generation of children is being raised by their grandparents, while parents are working. This has actually served to better preserve cultures, since the grandparents have time and opportunity to pass their language and customs on to the little ones. An increasing number of Indian-run educational and social services are also assuming mothers' traditional roles.

Mothers are traditionally associated with preparing food, and this is still the case in most Native communities throughout the Americas. A diet of processed foods, sugars, and fats has unfortunately taken the place of the healthy foods

Native people used to enjoy. This has caused much suffering from *diabetes* in Indian communities. In fact, American Indians are three times more likely to die from diabetes-related health problems than are Caucasian Americans.

Some rural Indians continue to hunt wild game to add to their family's food. Fishing is also a source of food for nations near rivers, and Native people continue to fight legal battles for the use and control of their own waterways. Native women living in rural areas are likely to be skilled in scaling, skinning, and butchering fish and game. In some cases, a spiritual element is still attached to harvesting wildlife. Women offer prayers of gratitude to the Creator and to the fallen creature before wildlife is butchered and eaten.

Native communities continue to struggle with a host of serious problems caused by centuries of mistreatment by the larger society. Drugs, alcohol, unemployment, and suicide all challenge young people's efforts to succeed in life. Mothers and the family structures they uphold continue to provide hope and strength for Indian nations.

"THE STORIES OF NATIVE AMERICAN MILITARY WOMEN ARE A UNIQUE AND IMPORTANT PART OF THE LARGER STORY OF WOMEN'S SERVICE TO THE NATION." —RETIRED AIR FORCE BRIGADIER GENERAL WILMA L. VAUGHT

5

HONORED OPPONENTS: NATIVE WOMEN IN THE MILITARY AND IN SPORTS

On March 23, 2003, a small convoy of American troops in the Iraqi desert took a fatal wrong turn. The 507th Maintenance Company drove into the outskirts of Nasiriyah—and into an Iraqi ambush. The brutal firefight that followed ended with fifteen American troops reported missing. One of these was Lori Piestewa, a twenty-three-year-old Hopi Indian and mother of two little children.

In Piestewa's hometown, Tuba City, Arizona, her clan and all the town's citizens held a *vigil*. Yellow ribbons hung from trees, cars, and signposts. Prayers were offered up in both Christian and traditional Indian fashion. Nine days later, the press reported that Jessica Lynch, who had been Lori's friend and roommate, had been rescued. That lifted everyone's hopes. But on April 4, those hopes were dashed. Piestewa's body was reported found in a shallow grave.

An article in the *Arizona Republic* newspaper, by reporters Pat Flannery and Betty Reid, tells the story of Piestewa's life. The article says:

> She loved her two kids, cooking chicken enchiladas, playing softball and listening to the Cranberries. She was a church-going Catholic, but she

honored her Hopi heritage by attending religious dances at nearby Moenkopi village. Most of all, she had aspirations.

She was born in 1980 to a Hopi father and a Latina mother. Her Hopi family name literally means, "pool of still water." In high school, she was called "Little Lori," but being short didn't stop her from being a competitive volleyball player. A teammate recalled, "She never gave up, she always tried harder." She was also involved in ROTC [Reserve Officers Training Corps], where she first became interested in the military.

Lori Piestewa graduated, married a Navajo man who was headed for military service, and had two children over the next two years. In 2001, she and her husband separated, and she decided to go into military service. Her decision was a painful one, as it meant the young mother would have to leave her two children while serving her country. The *Arizona Republic* article notes:

> An inordinate number of young Native Americans make the military their destination, if only short-term, because it offers instant money, free on-the-job training, decent benefits, a structured and patriotic environment and a line on the resumé that says "veteran." It gives them a leg up if they decide to compete for prized government jobs back home on "the rez."

Lori Piestewa was a young woman determined to make the most she could out of her life. As a result, she wound up earning a place in history as the first American Indian woman known to have died in combat serving with the United States Armed Forces. Her four-year-old son, Brandon, has a different understanding of his mother's fate. He told his father and grandmother, "My mom is an angel. I'll never see her again. She's an angel watching over you."

The United States Army has not documented any other Indian female having died in combat, but that may be due to poorly kept military records regard-

ing Native women in service. The idea of women warriors is hardly new among Native people. Several North American tribes have oral histories that tell of exceptional women fighting alongside men in the olden days.

There is a long record of Native women serving in the United States military, as well. Linda Hoffman reports on Indian women in the military in *Canku Ota: An Online Newsletter Celebrating Native America*. During World War I, fourteen American Indian women served in the Army Nurse Corp. During World War II, eight hundred American Indian women served in

A MOUNTAIN IN HER HONOR

Squaw Peak in north-central Phoenix will soon be renamed Piestewa Peak. The State Board on Geographic and Historic Names approved the change by a five-to-one vote before a cheering crowd. The board agreed with citizens who said the word "squaw" is offensive and the mountain should be renamed after Lori Piestewa. The Hopi from Tuba City was the first female American Indian soldier to be killed in combat.

Native women demonstrate the same pride in a powwow dance that they give to military service.

various roles. Today, there are more than 2,700 Native women in uniforms of the United States Armed Services.

Though they have served well and sacrificed much, American Indian women remain unsung heroes. For a long time, they have struggled against restrictions historically directed at women, as well as cultural barriers challenging Indians in the larger American society. Fortunately, today the armed services are making a determined effort to remove *discrimination*. Brigadier General LaRita Aragon of the Oklahoma Air National Guard is from the Cherokee and Choctaw nations. She was the first woman to reach such a high rank in the armed services. She says, "I believe the military is one of the greatest leveling fields for equality that there is."

A VERY OLD TRADITION

During the 1777 Revolutionary War battle of Oriskany in New York, Tyonajanegen, a member of the Oneida nation, fought valiantly beside her husband, an American Army officer. She stood by him firing at attacking British troops. She was the first American Indian woman to serve America in the military.

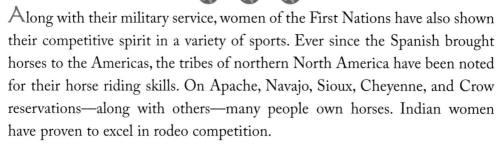

Along with their military service, women of the First Nations have also shown their competitive spirit in a variety of sports. Ever since the Spanish brought horses to the Americas, the tribes of northern North America have been noted for their horse riding skills. On Apache, Navajo, Sioux, Cheyenne, and Crow reservations—along with others—many people own horses. Indian women have proven to excel in rodeo competition.

Lynn McGuire is a member of the Osage tribe in the state of Oklahoma. She has won fourteen national finals, and in 1993, she became the only woman to ever qualify in the national finals for team roping. She is also a two-time world champion in steer roping, and she was named Miss Indian Rodeo.

Although it is not a sport, powwow dancing can be a form of competition, and requires considerable athletic skill. Powwows are cultural celebrations, popular throughout North America and Canada.

One category of competition is traditional dancing. Women's traditional dances are a display of physical strength, rhythm, and agility. Timed carefully with the drumbeats, dancers keep their steps close to the ground. Their regalia—traditional clothing for special occasions—are part of the event. This usually includes a fringed shawl and an eagle feather fan. Dresses may be made of colorful cloth or buckskins, decorated with beadwork, quillwork, and embroidery or elks' teeth buttons.

Another category is the women's Jingle Dance. Dresses are made of cloth, covered with jingles made of shiny metal. Between four hundred and seven hundred jingles adorn an adult jingle dress. As in other traditional dances, the dancers keep their feet close to the ground and pay careful attention to rhythm.

The women's fancy shawl dance is the most modern form of women's powwow dancing. The dance is highly athletic, including fast leaping and spinning

Lynn McGuire

This Native woman demonstrates her creativity and pride as she performs the fancy shawl dance at a powwow.

movements. Fancy shawl dancers wear brightly colored shawls and dresses, with extra long fringes. These dances are very creative and individualistic.

Throughout Western North America, basketball is a highly popular and competitive sport for Indians of both sexes. Peter Iverson, in his book *Diné*, says, "It seemed as though any home you visited in Navajo country had a basketball hoop. Future prospective National Basketball Association stars often learned to dribble on dirt."

Carolyn Jones writes in the *San Francisco Chronicle* about Jacqueline Sanchez, a University of California, Berkeley, basketball player, member of the Paiute and Shoshone tribes and *mentor* to American Indian students. Sanchez progressed from being a star basketball player at Mira Loma High School in Sacramento, to junior college and then University of California, Berkeley. She credits the support she found through her teammates and American Indian student groups for her success. Sanchez says:

> Basketball is a really big thing for Native Americans. It's an easy thing for us to get involved in because you don't need a field, you don't need money for equipment. All you need is a ball and a hoop. We all play a lot.

Down in Mexico, girls excel at a very different sport that also involves a rubber ball—a game that was the ancient ancestor of today's internationally popular pastime. The ancient Aztec ball game, Ulama, is the distant ancestor of today's basketball. In ornately decorated ball courts, teams of warrior athletes battled to place hard rubber balls through the hoops, using only their hips to move the ball. Losing teams were killed by ritual sacrifice. Even in ancient times, when competition was deadly serious, there were teams of female players.

Today, the ancient tradition continues with a game called *Ulama de Antebrazo*. In this game, a smaller hard rubber ball is played back and forth using only the forearms. Dulce Villa, a thirteen-year-old Mexican girl, is the

Dulce Villa uses her forearm to deflect a small rubber ball in Ulama de Antebrazo.

star of the sport. She comes from a long tradition of female players. An article in the September 2003 issue of *Archaeology* magazine notes how she plays, "with fierce intensity, regularly beating boys her age and older."

In military service, in the rodeo, in the powwow dance circle, and on the ball court, Native women throughout the Americas have proven their athletic and competitive abilities. They continue the traditions begun by warrior women and athletes of the past, and excel in modern forms of sport as well. They honor their nations and their families as proud competitors.

ANOTHER AMERICAN INDIAN CONTRIBUTION

Lacrosse is a sport enjoyed by thousands of men and women, boys and girls across North America. Queen Victoria of England declared lacrosse to be Canada's national sport after a traveling team of Mohawks introduced it to excited crowds in England. For the six nations of the Haudenosaunee (Iroquois), lacrosse is part of their Creation traditions.

"AS LONG AS YOU KEEP A GOOD HEART, YOU ALWAYS WIN. BECAUSE GOOD OVERCOMES EVIL."
—VERNA WILLIAMSON

WISE LEADERS: NATIVE WOMEN TODAY IN TRIBAL AND POLITICAL LEADERSHIP

Verna Williamson became governor of Isleta Pueblo in 1986, the first woman governor of any Pueblo Indian tribe. Her optimism has enabled her to overcome many difficulties and improve the lives of people in Isleta. In recent years, she has forced the Environmental Protection Agency to clean up the Rio Grande River, which runs through her village. Williamson has been described as tough yet compassionate, traditional yet able to work effectively in the modern political world. Before running for governor, she sought the advice of her tribal elders. They told her, "The government came to us from the Spanish. This is recent history, only three or four hundred years ago." They said there was no reason that ancient sacred ways would prohibit her from running for office.

Women have had an extraordinary effect on the leadership of North America's indigenous communities. Of all the tribal nations in the United States, the Cherokees are recognized as one of the best organized. They have a strong economy, an efficient governmental structure, and they are largely self-sufficient. The driving force given credit for many of their successes is a female chief—Wilma Mankiller.

NATURAL LAW

"In all countries, real wealth stems from the control of land and its resources. Our Iroquois philosophers knew this as well as we knew natural law. To us it made sense for women to control the land since they were far more sensitive to the rhythms of the Mother Earth."

—Doug George-Kanentiio, **Iroquois Culture & Commentary**

Mankiller was raised on a farm in eastern Oklahoma. Her family then moved to California. In the 1960s, she and other family members became involved in the Indian rights movement. After she finished her college education, Mankiller moved back to Oklahoma. She threw herself into improving the community where she was born. She worked hard to make connections between the tribal government and traditional-minded Cherokee people who lived in the country. She was so successful, the people asked her to run for deputy chief of the Cherokee Nation.

In 1983, she ran for the office of Principle Chief. Some Cherokees were upset with the idea of a female chief; she actually received death threats during the campaign. When she won, that made her the leader of the largest Indian nation in the United States. Mankiller has described the job of Principle Chief

as being like "running a small country, a medium-sized corporation, and being a social worker." When Mankiller left the chief's office in 1995, she had made significant and lasting changes for the good of the Cherokee people.

Among the Apache tribes, women have always played a strong role in social life. It is no surprise, then, that two Apache tribes now have woman presidents. Sara Misquez has helped the Mescalero Nation experience solid business growth. The Mescalero Tribe recently completed a $34-million-dollar school, which is state-of-the-art. A state official claims, "There's not any facility better in the nation."

Claudia Vigil-Muniz is the first woman president of the Jicarilla Apache Nation. A sign in her office says, "Women make great leaders: You're following one now." The mother of two grown children, she ran in 2000 for president with vice presidential running mate Lamavaya Caramillo. Caramillo is known for being traditional in her approach to things, and she nicely balances Vigil-Muniz, who received a college education off the reservation. Vigil-Muniz is careful to respect tribal traditions. She fully supports the continuation of sacred Jicarilla rituals, which separate the roles of men and women.

Geri Small was elected president of the Northern Cheyenne Nation in 2000. Her Indian name means, "Thunder and Lightning Woman," which is fitting for a woman who has made some impressive achievements. She is the first woman president to lead a tribe in Montana and Wyoming.

She is not, however, the first female leader of the Cheyenne. In the 1800s, a woman named North Woman gave direction to her tribe—just as the North Star gives directions to travelers. She helped lead the people from Oklahoma, where they were being held, to their ancestral lands in Montana. She was a medicine woman, and oral histories tell of her leading her people through a net of hostile soldiers, relying on the power of supernatural visions she received. In the past one hundred years, however, the Northern Cheyenne did not have women leaders—until Geri Small.

Acoma women no longer dress as they did when Edward Curtis took this picture in 1904—but they still have the same political power they have wielded since pre-Columbian times.

YOU'VE COME A LONG WAY—BACKWARD!

"The traditional system of government and equality between the sexes were lost temporarily during the change to reservation life; this process meant that Indian culture was often devalued. Women were not allowed to participate in politics."

—Karen Lonehill, in the Mason Crest book, **Sioux**

Gail Small, Geri's sister, is another sort of leader. She has been an activist for environmental causes. Gail describes what Geri is doing as reservation president: "trying to rebuild the entire reservation water system. . . roads and *infrastructure* . . . we're rebuilding a nation from the ground up."

Several nations of North American Indians continue their ancient traditions of giving great responsibility and authority to the older women who lead their clans. The Haudenosaunee (Iroquois) are a confederacy, a group of six united nations. Each nation has a council of chiefs, chosen by the clan mothers. The clan mothers select chiefs and councilmen. They also sit with the chiefs and councilmen and discuss issues with them. The clan mothers don't vote, but they have the power to remove the councilmen if they think the men aren't doing their jobs responsibly. Brian Patterson, who is a council member of the Oneida

ANOTHER DEBT TO NATIVE PEOPLE

Ironically, while the U.S. government was creating a new system of reservation government that took power away from female leaders, Iroquois women were influencing other women in the United States to achieve equal rights. In 1914, a publication dedicated to the goal of women voting printed the following:

We, the women of the Iroquois

Own the land, the lodge, the children;

Ours is the right to raise up and depose chiefs;

Ours is the right to representation at all councils;

Our lives are valued as high as man's.

Nation, says, "The clan mothers are the heart and soul of our nation, the true leaders of our people."

At Acoma Pueblo, in New Mexico, men do the work of government, yet they serve at the pleasure of the clan mothers. The women of the Antelope Clan appoint tribal officers: the Governor, Lieutenant Governor, Secretary, Treasurer, and so on. If they wish, the men appointed may leave office after

their term has expired. They may also be removed if the clan mothers perceive them to be failing in their duties.

Throughout North America, women not only serve as elected political leaders, they also have made a significant impact on the world as activists. Winona LaDuke is a notable example. She is a 1982 graduate of Harvard who now lives on the White Earth Reservation in Minnesota. In 1994, *Time* magazine named her as one of America's fifty most promising leaders under forty years of age. In 2000, she ran as vice president on the ticket with Ralph Nader, for the Green Party.

Jay Walljasper interviewed her for *Mother Jones* magazine in January of 1996. He reports that LaDuke grew up on the West Coast with her Anishinabe father and Jewish mother. She moved to White Earth, in Minnesota, after completing her degree at Harvard. She was determined to recover lands that were promised to the Anishinabe people in an 1867 treaty. Over 90 percent of the original 837,000 acres are in the hands of non-Indians. To gain these lands back, she founded the White Earth Land Recovery Project. Using grants, the group has bought back more than 1,000 acres.

LaDuke finds strength in her traditional Anishinabe spiritual beliefs. "Spirituality is the foundation of all my political work. . . . What we all need to do is find the wellspring that keeps us going, that gives us the strength and patience to keep up this struggle for a long time."

At the beginning of the twenty-first century, American Indian women are showing no shortage of strength or patience. Clan mothers, tribal chieftains, activists, and other Native women leaders continue to display impressive achievements as they guide their people toward a brighter future.

SKILLED HANDS:
NATIVE WOMEN ARTISTS

Like many of her people, Dana Tiger has gone through suffering and struggles—yet her hard experiences have enabled her to create objects of special beauty. Her life and work are described in Autumn Libal's book, *Creek*, in Mason Crest's NORTH AMERICAN INDIANS TODAY series. A descendant of Creek, Seminole, and Cherokee nations, Dana Tiger is an award-winning artist from Oklahoma. When she was a little girl, she lost her father to an accidental shooting. He left her a legacy, however—artwork that inspired her to create. Her father's work is highly regarded today.

Later in life, more tragedies struck Dana Tiger. Her brother was murdered, and not too long after, her sister was diagnosed with HIV. Dana Tiger was herself diagnosed in 2000 with Parkinson's disease, an illness that attacks the victim's muscles.

Dana Tiger's paintings depict Native American women who have overcome challenges, who have bettered their world. She says, "By realizing the natural strength and courage of women in my ancestry, I hope to portray the historical dignity and contemporary determination of Native American women."

Native women in the Americas are known for their outstanding contributions to the art world—both in contemporary *mediums*, such as Dana Tiger's paintings, and in age-old forms such as weaving and pottery. In traditional culture, the beautiful things people made weren't thought of as "art." Most objects now considered art were practical in nature—blankets, cooking or storage utensils, clothing, and so on. Decorations—painting, beadwork, pottery, intricate woven designs—were regarded as qualities of skillfully made objects.

Many Indian people today sell craftwork to supplement their incomes. They have learned through the years not to depend on jobs that come from agencies or companies off tribal lands. Such jobs come and go. Meanwhile, artistic skills

IF YOU'VE GOT IT, YOU'LL KNOW IT

"I started to weave when I was six. My grandma was going blind. One day she couldn't see and she said, 'It's your turn. There is no other way we can get food.' She didn't teach me, she just said, 'You've seen me weave all these years; you should know if you've got it in you.'"

—Weaver Kalley Musial, quoted in Stephen Trimble's **The People**

Indigenous girls in Guatemala continue to weave beautiful designs using backstrap loom techniques similar to those of their ancestors in pre-Columbian times.

enable Native women to provide for their families when other work is unavailable.

Navajo (or Diné) weaving is one of the most highly prized forms of North American Indian artistry. Diné weavers are traditionally female. Raymond Locke, in *The Book of the Navajo*, recalls the words of a European lady watching a Diné woman weaving. She said, "It is the handiwork of the gods." That description may be literally true in the minds of the Diné. According to the Navajo's traditions, Spider Woman, a powerful supernatural being, taught the Diné how to weave. In the past, Diné women would leave a hole in the center of each blanket, like that in a spider's web. Traders in the early twentieth century would not buy blankets with holes in them, so Navajo weavers came up with a different custom. Today, each weaving has a "spirit outlet," which is a thin line from the center of the blanket to the edge. If such a spirit outlet is not included, Spider Woman will inflict the user with "blanket sickness" or mental confusion.

To make fine blankets, the wool must first be trimmed off the sheep. The Navajo raise churro sheep especially for this purpose. Then the wool must be carded and spun into yarn. This is done with a hand spindle, which looks like

ART WITH SOUL

If you acquire a handmade Pueblo Indian pot you are getting more than hardened clay—traditional potters truly put themselves into their art. Ruth Koyona, of Laguna Pueblo, says, "I talk to my pots. When it goes, I tell it 'Go with this person—they will love you like I did. My spirit goes with the person.'"

NATIVE WOMEN IN THE AMERICAS

a big top rotated on the floor. Dyes are made from plants: chamizo flowers are boiled to make a deep yellow; rabbit bush makes an earthy yellow; and prickly pear cactus makes a rose or purple dye.

Blankets are woven on an upright loom. It takes two to three months to weave a four-foot-by-six-foot rug, or five to six months for an extremely fine piece. Non-Native people, used to machine-made products, sometimes think hand-woven tapestries are expensive. Diné weavers are really asking very little for their work, when one considers the time involved.

D. Y. Begay is a noted Navajo weaver. In May of 2000, Begay and another Diné woman traveled to an indigenous community in Guatemala. Guatemala's Indians are, like the Navajo, famous for woven art. Begay exchanged techniques with women of the Q'uechi tribe. Guatemala's Mayan women still make clothing, tapestries, and items of apparel using techniques practiced by their ancestors before the Spanish came to this continent. Their designs are bright and intricate. Women of Guatemala's highlands wear beautiful handmade blouses and skirts, either for everyday wear or more commonly, for dress occasions. While Navajo weavers use an upright loom, framed by sturdy wooden posts, Mayan weavers use a backstrap loom, which is held taut by a belt tied around the weaver's waist and attached on the other end to a tree. Although they did not speak each other's languages, the Q'uechi and Navajo women enjoyed sharing techniques. Begay has also traveled to Peru and Spain to meet and exchange skills with other weavers. The Diné have been exchanging artistic techniques with other cultures for centuries, and now in the twenty-first century that exchange has become global.

The Indians of the twenty U.S. pueblos of Arizona and New Mexico are famous for their pottery. The majority of potters are women, though some men are noted for their artistry with clay, and there are also couples who produce pottery together. Clay bowls, jars, and canteens express elements of life that are very important to traditional Pueblo Indians. These containers hold water, which is the most valued life-giving substance for people who have lived for centuries in the desert. Seed pots and jars contained corn, the staple of agricultural life. Clay itself is a gift from Earth to her children.

Until the last century, non-Indian society had little appreciation for Pueblo pottery. That changed in 1915, when San Ildefonso potter Maria Martinez gained fame at the San Diego World's fair. She and her husband Julian created a beautiful, shiny black style of pottery. Artists and collectors clamored for their work. Around the same time, Hopi potter Nampeyo gained international attention for her ceramic creations. The fame of these two potters led to a worldwide market for Pueblo Indian pottery.

The first step in Pueblo pottery making is gathering clay. Each potter has her favorite site. Prayers and corn offerings are made to thank Mother Earth. As a further sign of respect, hand tools are used to remove the clay.

MORE THAN JUST PRETTY

"The symbols and patterns on everything from pots to footwear allow artists and people to reflect on the world around them and to be reminded of its . . . significance."
—Larry Zimmerman, Native North American

Many Native women, like the Seminole of Florida and Oklahoma, are skilled seamstresses.

This Pueblo woman proudly displays her people's bead and silver handiwork.

The significance of designs in American Indian art is not always immediately obvious. For example, animal designs often represent the various clans and their roles in society. Geometric designs on southwest ceramics represent clouds, rain, and lightning—a reminder of the importance of water in a desert environment.

The clay is then soaked in water to get an even consistency. *Temper* is added to the clay to strengthen it. Ruth Koyona, of Laguna Pueblo, actually gathers broken pieces of pottery left centuries ago by her ancient ancestors, and grinds them to temper her clay. The lucky person who gets one of Ruth's pots is actually buying a piece of today's art and pieces of the past combined into one. After adding temper, the clay is shaped. Traditional Pueblo potters do not use a potter's wheel. The clay is pinched into shape, and smoothed with gourds. The clay is then set aside to dry.

After drying, color finishes are applied to the surface of the pot. Glazes are made from plants or minerals. Designs have traditional significance. Animal forms often represent clans. Brushes used to paint the designs are made of horsehair or yucca cactus leaves.

Finally, the pottery must be fired. Firing is a complex task. A beehive-shaped structure is made of sheep manure, and a grate placed on top of that. This is covered with large pieces of broken pottery, and another layer of manure is placed on that. Firing takes three hours, and must be done perfectly or the pots will shatter.

Innumerable forms of indigenous art are being produced by women throughout the Americas, from fine fabrics and pottery produced in the tropical Amazon jungles, to delicate ivory carvings made by the Inuit on the frozen Arctic shore. The Sioux, Crow, Northern Cheyenne, and other Plains tribes create quilted blankets, leather dresses decorated with fine beadwork or designs made from dyed quills, lavishly decorated cradleboards, and other objects of fine art. Tribes in California, Mexico, and Arizona continue the arts of weaving grass or horsehair into baskets.

While Native arts are flourishing today, at the same time Indian artists find their livelihoods threatened by sales of imitations. It has been roughly estimated that sales of Indian crafts each year in America may amount to a billion dollars. Tragically, more than half those sales go to non-Indian fakers. Counterfeit Indian arts are made in Pakistan, India, Thailand, and the Philippines. These fakes are then sold as genuine Indian art. Counterfeiting Indian art is not only morally wrong; it can be devastating to Native people's lives. For some Indian artists, lost sales means their cars have been repossessed, and in worse cases, utilities shut off in their homes.

If you buy Indian art, make sure it is actually made by Native artists. Many fakes are marketed through the mail or Internet as "Indian made." The surest way to buy the genuine article is to buy directly from the artist. Ask for a receipt stating the name of the artist and the tribe he or she is part of. And remember that age-old piece of advice—if something looks too good to be true,

NATIVE WOMEN IN THE AMERICAS

it probably is. Handmade Native artwork takes time and skill to make; it is seldom sold for "rock-bottom" prices.

Along with the visual arts, Native women in the Americas excel in performance art as well. Women's skills in powwow dancing have been noted in chapter 5. Others have achieved success in ballet. Melissa Wishinski, a Cherokee, became a world-class ballerina while still in her teens. Maria Tallchief, of the Osage, was a member of the New York City ballet for almost two decades.

Indian women have also found success as musicians and singers. Joanne Shenandoah, a Wolf Clan member of the Oneida, is an award-winning composer and singer. She combines traditional Haudenosaunee (Iroquois) songs with modern musical effects. Noted for her outstanding voice, she has performed at the White House and at President Clinton's inauguration.

Jana, a member of the Lumbee Tribe of North Carolina, has achieved success recording and performing techno-style dance tracks. She also sells her own line of jewelry, and is filming a movie. While thoroughly modern in her artistic expressions, she also participates in traditional Lumbee dances and ceremonies. Jana embodies the Lumbee saying, "She walks in beauty in two worlds."

Today, Native women throughout the Americas contribute their talents in a wide variety of arts—traditional and contemporary, visual, practical, and performance. Their flourishing artistic achievements reflect the continuing strength and important contributions of First Nations people to the rest of the world.

"IN EFFECT, WOMEN HAVE BEEN, AND REMAIN, THE KEEPERS OF THEIR CULTURE, PRESERVING TRADITIONS AND HANDING THEM DOWN TO THEIR CHILDREN."
—RAYNA GREEN

8

NOURISHING SOULS: HEALERS, MENTORS, AND KEEPERS OF TRADITION

Lori Arviso Alvord has found strength by relating to a story of her Diné (Navajo) people. The story tells of a young woman whose husband is killed by enemies. Coyote enabled her to turn into a ferocious bear. In this form, she is able to take vengeance on those who had caused her grief. Afterward, she becomes a woman again. This oral tradition reminded Alvord of her strength, as a woman descended from the Bear Clan. Bear-like courage and *tenacity* enabled her to become the first Navajo woman surgeon.

She grew up on the Navajo reservation, the daughter of a Diné man and a blond-haired, blue-eyed mother. She tells in her book, *The Scalpel and the Silver Bear*, of the difficulties growing up between two worlds—Navajo and white. She excelled at school, and with the encouragement of a medical researcher, went to medical school.

Her time there was extremely difficult for a person raised with traditional Diné beliefs. The Navajo will never touch a corpse—or even go near one. A dead body disrupts the harmony necessary for health and good fortune. Yet to become a physician, she had to dissect cadavers, and break other *taboos*. As a

"In traditional Iroquois society, every individual had guaranteed health care, which began at birth and carried on until death. Within any given Iroquois community, there were a number of people actively involved in administering to the health needs of its members. There were practitioners who functioned as dieticians, psychologists, midwives, herbalists, and physicians, all working in concert to heal mind, body, and spirit."

—Doug George-Kanentiio, **Iroquois Culture & Commentary**

training physician, she worked herself to exhaustion and became infected with a disease that might well have killed her. Still, she persevered.

After passing medical school, she was able to fulfill her lifelong dream of returning to the Navajo Reservation as a surgeon. There, she encountered problems unusual to the rest of the world—people whose experiences included supernatural threats, epidemic rates of diabetes and alcoholism, and rare diseases unique to this isolated part of America. An extremely rare and deadly plague broke out on the Navajo reservation and nearby parts of Arizona. Modern scientists searched frantically for its cause. A *medicine man* told a researcher that

Native women have a long tradition of leadership. These Mayan ruins portray a woman who led her people around A.D. 780.

Pueblo children learn the dance traditions of their people.

he had seen a similar illness long ago, and it had been stopped by a ceremony, which included a sandpainting portraying mice. "Look to the mice," said the medicine man. Sure enough, a virus found in rodent droppings caused the deadly disease.

From her experiences in her Navajo nation, Lori Arviso Alvord began to make connections that would revolutionize her own—and others'—understanding of medicine and health. The Diné concept of life places great importance on *hózhó*, the idea that "everything in life is connected and influences everything else." Sickness, according to the Navajo, can be caused by nonphysical aspects of life being out of order. Unhealthy relationships, spiritual problems, or emotional problems cause illness. Alvord began to apply the concept of hózhó to her medical practice. She found that if she established a relationship with her patient before practice, the surgery would go better. If the medical team performing a surgery spoke kindly with one another, that also helped. She

THE BEST OF BOTH WORLDS

"Some illnesses doctors can cure; some illnesses traditional medicine can cure; some can be helped by both; some can be helped by neither."

—Rose Hulligan, Navajo, quoted in Stephen Trimble's **The People** also began urging patients to include traditional Navajo healing rituals—such as the Night Chant Ceremony—along with medicine as part of the healing process.

Lori Arviso Alvord says in her book, "By implementing certain Navajo ways, I believe doctors can achieve better results in their practices. Living between two worlds, and never quite belonging to either, I have learned from both."

Before modern medicine existed, American Indian women combined spiritual concepts with a detailed knowledge of natural remedies to heal sicknesses among their people. Colonial settlers and trappers knew they would be more

THE END RESULT

"Native ceremonies have an end, they have closure. The ceremony returns patients to harmony, gives them the strength and right frame of mind to heal themselves, reaffirms the person's value, and reinstates them in the community. In western medicine, closure comes when the bill arrives!"
—Jennie Joe, Navajo, in Stephen Trimble's **The People**

likely to heal if they were treated by Native medicine people, rather than the crude and ineffective techniques of European doctors of that time. Many medicines used today to treat sickness around the world were first used by Native American healers. Today, it is becoming commonplace to combine First Nations' traditional wisdom with medical healing. Prayer, chants, and traditional herbal remedies are encouraged in modern hospitals on many North American Indian reservations.

The medicine wheel is a concept increasingly applied to healing. This is a hoop, divided into four sections, which are the mental, physical, emotional, and spiritual principles in life. These four united principles have been useful in developing Native medical practices, as well as counseling for drug and alcohol addictions.

Since ancient times, Native women have served their communities as healers of the people, and keepers of traditions. To *Western* thinking, these things don't seem to go together. Yet to Native thought, the harmony of a community and its physical health are closely tied together.

Long Standing Bear Chief, a writer, educator, and lecturer, is a member of the Blackfoot Nation. He writes in an article for the *Yakima Herald*:

> Women have always been important and have had a prominent role in the life of our people. The spirit and the power of the female is prayed for and to, in order that their power will help us, and thereby save us, our world, and our universe.

One way Native women today are healing and renewing their world is the Braveheart Society. Brenda Norrel describes its contribution in an article for *Canku Ota: An Online Newsletter Celebrating Native America*. The Braveheart Society began as an effort by grandmothers of the Yankton Sioux tribe in South Dakota, to mentor younger women. At their first *retreat*, they discovered that

many Native girls needed healing from physical and sexual abuse. They now conduct retreats regularly, to heal and renew younger women with companionship, awareness, and traditional healing practices. Faith Spotted Eagle, one of the group's founders, says, "Our cultures have remedies for all of us." Another way the Braveheart Society builds self-esteem is by conducting coming-of-age ceremonies. They also share traditional stories, teach how to plant and grow healthy foods, and perform dramas portraying problems and healing within families.

In the past, families and clans passed on values to American Indian children. Today, family and clan have diminished in importance. As parents increasingly work outside of the home, and as poverty and resulting social problems break up homes, institutions have become more important in caring for children. Boys and Girls Clubs offer many services that help shape the coming generations of Native young people. Women continue to play the major role in these settings as well.

Jeanetta Wobig is unit director for the Hardin, Montana, Boys & Girls Club. The club promotes understanding of Crow culture, drug awareness and *abstinence*, alcohol abuse prevention, and it enables Native and non-Native kids to interact with one another with better understanding. Equipped with ten computers and an Internet satellite dish, the club helps children with their homework. They also do community service, like cleaning up litter and serving food at the Crow Tribal Fair. Jeanetta is constantly at the club, trying to expand its services for the children of the Crow Nation. She is typical of the many Native women who are dedicated to helping young people get a positive start in life.

For thousands of years, American Indian women communicated values and beliefs through the spoken word. Today, a number of female Native authors

have earned recognition for their words put into print. Leslie Marmon Silko, of Laguna Pueblo, has gained critical acclaim for her writing. At the same time, many Indian people in North America believe that the spoken word is still the appropriate way to convey important lessons through the generations. Audrey Wong, writing for *Canku Ota*, tells how "The California Indian Storytelling Festivals provide a gathering place where California Indian storytellers . . . present workshops, panel discussions, and storytelling performances—a time when the stories, in both traditional form and contemporary experience, may flourish." In 2003, thirty-eight storytellers from more than twenty tribes, spoke at the event. California tribes present included the Ohlone, Chumash, Pit River, and Hupa. One storyteller even came from Costa Rica.

Clarence Hostler, of the Hupa and Karuk tribes, shared traditional teachings about how emotional troubles in the home can harm children. "The child who can't cope with problems at home can bring those problems to society. It can contaminate the community. It can extend to gangs and terrorism." Hostler says, "Stories and philosophies centuries old can still pertain to modern life."

THE SEVENTH GENERATION:
LOOKING TOWARD THE FUTURE

The number seven has special significance to indigenous American cultures. Many Indians speak of having special responsibilities to the people who will come after them, "down to the seventh generation." The Mohawk, Anishinabe (Iroquois) and Oceti Sakowin (Sioux) people recall prophecies regarding the seventh generation from the arrival of white settlers to their lands. The prophecies predicted years of terrible suffering and turmoil. In the seventh generation, however, the earth will be restored to harmony and indigenous people will regain their lands, rights, and respect. Curiously, Native Hawaiians have a similar prophecy. For many Native young people, theirs is the seventh generation. What does the world look like as this generation approaches adulthood? Throughout the Americas, Native women continue to struggle. Women in all North American societies continue to lag behind men in terms of income. Indigenous women face disadvantages on the basis of their gender, as well as race and culture. In North America, there are still Indian reservations with 90 percent unemployment rates. Epidemic levels of alcoholism and diabetes afflict many Indian nations.

Professor Dale Old Horn, of Crow Nation Little Bighorn College, explains that the destruction of their traditional cultures has caused loss of identity for some American Indians. This in turn leads to "alcohol abuse, drug abuse, spouse abuse, child abuse and gambling addictions."

Isolated and traditional Native communities are threatened by *ecological* developments. Oil drilling in the arctic wilderness threatens caribou herds, which indigenous hunters still depend upon. The Tarahumara Indians in Mexico's Sierra Mountains see their lands destroyed by logging and illegal drug farming. The Amazon rain forests disappear, and loggers and miners bring diseases and violence to hidden jungle communities. In rural communities of Central and South America, indigenous people suffer from malnutrition, high rates of death in childbirth, and death from diseases that are curable but untreated.

Despite such grim realities, there is nonetheless reason for optimism. The seventh generation may yet fulfill their prophesied destiny. In North America, young Indian women are better educated than their mothers' or grandmothers' generations. At the same time, many young women also have a strong sense of loyalty to their Native traditions. Native language lessons, participation in traditional ceremonies, and Indian spiritual practices are increasingly popular. For centuries now, Native women have struggled to balance their cultural identities between the white and Indian worlds. The latest generation of young people seems comfortable achieving success in both.

The achievements of young Native women may not be of the dramatic, headline-grabbing sort, but they are significant. In Aniak, Alaska, girls from thirteen to twenty years old form the Dragonslayers, a volunteer medical rescue team. The girls carry beepers to their classes, and are allowed to leave without question for emergencies. The community was lacking adequate volunteers for an emergency team, so these young women stepped up to fill the need. They have saved many lives.

Throughout the Americas, many Native people, like these children in Campeche, Mexico, face poverty, discrimination, and other challenges.

Young Native women may be the prophesied seventh generation—the ones who will restore harmony for their people and healing for the world.

On Montana's Crow nation, four eighth-grade girls from Pretty Eagle Catholic School beat out thousands of competitors in the Bayer National Science Foundation Competition. The countrywide competition challenges students to find scientific approaches to community needs. The girls, who named their team "The Rez Protectors," demonstrated the practicality of building with cement-covered straw bales to help ease a housing shortage on their reservation. They later appeared on *Oprah Winfrey* and the *Today Show*, as well as a conference sponsored by Vice President Al Gore.

Young women are also making a difference in the village of Todos Santos, in northwest Guatemala's highlands, where women are a majority. Government soldiers killed large numbers of indigenous men in the 1980s, and the males who survived have left the village, looking for employment in the big cities and in the United States. It looked like the village might die out altogether, but the women have determined to save their community. The women have formed co-operatives, such as *Grupo de Mujeres*, to develop **cottage industries** and attract tourists to their village. The teen girls of the village are gaining an education, enabling them to achieve even more success in developing the local economy. Koren Capozza writes in *Horizon Magazine*, "The word on the street in Todos Santos is that the future is in women's hands and those hands are more than capable."

FURTHER READING

Arviso Alvord, Lori. *The Scalpel and the Silver Bear*. New York: Bantam, 2000.

Crow Dog, Mary. *Lakota Woman*. New York: Harper Collins, 1990.

Driving Hawk Sneve, Virginia. *Completing the Circle*. Lincoln: University of Nebraska Press, 1995.

George-Kanentiio, Doug. *Iroquois Culture & Commentary*. Santa Fe: Clear Light, 2000.

Green, Rayna. *Women in American Indian Society*. New York: Chelsea House, 1990.

Hazen-Hammond, Susan. *Spider Woman's Web*. New York: Berkley Publishing, 1999.

Hungry Wolf, Beverly. *The Ways of My Grandmothers*. New York: William Morrow, 1990.

Mankiller, Wilma. *Mankiller: A Chief and Her People*. New York: St. Martin's, 1993.

Libal, Autumn. *Creek*. Philadelphia: Mason Crest, 2004.

Lonehill, Karen. *Sioux*. Philadelphia: Mason Crest, 2004.

McIntosh, Kenneth. *Iroquois*. Philadelphia: Mason Crest, 2004.

———. *Pueblo*. Philadelphia: Mason Crest, 2004.

Marmon-Silko, Leslie. *Yellow Woman and Beauty of the Spirit*. New York: Simon & Schuster, 1996.

Stewart, Philip. *Osage*. Philadelphia: Mason Crest, 2004.

Time-Life editors. *The Woman's Way*. Alexandria, Va.: Time-Life, 1995.

Trimble, Stephen. *The People*. Santa Fe: SAR Press, 1993.

FOR MORE INFORMATION

Canku Ota (Many Paths): An Online Newsletter Celebrating Native America
www.turtletrack.org/

Peace for Turtle Island (Haudenosaunee/Iroquois nations links)
www.peace4turtleisland.org/

First Nations Site Index
www.dickshovel.com/www.html

Wotanging Ikche: Native American News
www.nanews.org/index2.shtml

Native Culture
www.nativeculture.com

Publisher's note:
The Web sites listed on this page were active at the time of publication. The publisher is not responsible for Web sites that have changed their addresses or discontinued operation since the date of publication. The publisher will review and update the Web sites upon each reprint.

GLOSSARY

abstinence Self-restraint, especially from indulgence in a craving.

activist Someone who practices direct action, especially in support of or opposition to one side of a controversial issue.

advocacy The act of supporting a cause.

anthropologists People who study the science of humans, especially in relation to distribution, origin, classification, and relationship of races, physical character, environmental and social relations, and culture.

breech birth A complication that can occur during childbirth where the baby is feet first in the birth canal rather than head first.

conquistador A conqueror; a sixteenth-century leader in the conquest of the Americas, especially of Mexico and Peru.

conversion An experience associated with an adoption of a religion.

cottage industries An early modern system of production, whereby goods such as shoes, leather goods, and pots were made at home.

diabetes Any of various abnormal conditions, whereby the inadequate use or secretion of insulin creates excessive urine production, too much sugar in the blood and urine, and causes thirst, hunger, and weight loss.

discrimination Treating people favorably or unfairly based on something that makes them distinct, such as their race, rather than their individual merit.

ecological Of or relating to the branch of science concerned with the interrelationships of organisms and their environments.

environmentalists People concerned with the quality of Earth's environment, especially regarding pollution.

epidemic A sudden rapid outbreak, growth, or development of contagious disease.

erotic Strongly affected or marked by sexual desire.

indigenous Native to a particular region or environment

infrastructure The basic framework or foundation of a system.

lobbyists People engaged in promoting or securing the passage of legislation by influencing public officials.

medicine man A priestly healer or sorcerer among Native Americans.

mediums People held to be a channel of communication between the spirit and earthly worlds.

mentor A trusted counselor, teacher, or coach.

midwives Women who assist other women in childbirth.

New-Agers People interested in Eastern culture, techniques of meditation, and methods for increasing consciousness and spirituality, who are also disenchanted with Western culture's emphasis on the materialistic.

polygamy Marriage in which a spouse of either sex has more than one mate at the same time.

retreat A period of group withdrawal for prayer, study, meditation, and instruction under a director.

revitalization The act or process of giving renewed vigor or life to something.

secular Relating to earthly life rather than spiritual.

smallpox A highly infectious disease that is caused by a poxvirus and believed to be wiped out due to vaccination.

stereotyped Conformed to a fixed pattern, especially a mental picture held in common by members of a group and representing an oversimplified opinion, prejudiced attitude, or uncritical judgment.

taboos Bans or prohibitions resulting from social custom.

temper To dilute, qualify, or soften by adding something else.

tenacity The quality or state of being persistent in adhering to something valued.

trafficker One buying and selling or bartering a usually illegal or disreputable commercial activity.

vigil An act or period of devotion, surveillance, or watching.

Western Of or relating to the culture of Europe and the United States.

INDEX

PICTURE CREDITS

Artville: p. 6
Michelle Bouch: pp. 10, 22, 34, 37, 41, 46, 48, 51, 56, 59, 68, 76, 88, 98, 102
© Philip Baird/www.anthroarcheart.org: pp. 12, 20, 32, 38, 44, 78, 91, 101
Edward Curtis, courtesy of: pp. 15, 25, 26, 30, 72
Corel: pp. 52, 84
Photos.com: pp. 60, 64, 83
Benjamin Stewart: p. 63, 92

BIOGRAPHIES

Kenneth McIntosh is a former schoolteacher and freelance writer, currently living in upstate New York. He has a bachelor's in English from Michigan State University, and taught junior high school for more than a decade in Los Angeles. He has had a lifelong interest in the indigenous people of the Western Hemisphere. In college, he spent a summer volunteering with youth at an American Indian community in British Columbia. More recently, he and his wife co-authored and researched six books for the Mason Crest series North American Indians Today. This project involved travel and interviews with people in more than a dozen Native American nations.

Dr. Mary Jo Dudley is the director of Cornell University's Gender and Global Change Department, which focuses on the evolving role of gender around the world. She is also the associate director of Latin American Studies at Cornell.